The Rain Girl

by Frances Usher

Illustrated by David Cuzik

Chapter 1

Nobody Will Come Now

If there was one thing that Rick and Anne-Marie didn't like, it was rain. Heavy, cold rain. It kept the punters away.

"Oh, no, look," groaned Rick one night, coming out of the caravan. "It's tipping down."

They hurried past the helter-skelter. Anne-Marie's dad waved to them. He made a rude face at the rain and laughed.

"Mind you don't get washed away," her mum shouted.

"People will come," said Rick. "They always do."

"A few," said Anne-Marie. "But rain is bad news round a fair. Tonight's going to be a bad night. I can feel it."

Anne-Marie had been born into the fair. She'd lived in it all her life. When she first left school, she'd worked on the helter-skelter with her mum and dad. But now she was working the dodgems with Rick. That was different. That was exciting.

But they needed the punters. And punters just didn't turn up when it rained. Without them, there'd be no money. Then where would they all be?

They reached the dodgems. "Come on, Rick, let's open up," said Anne-Marie. "I'll switch the music on. That will bring them in."

Rick started pushing the cars into line. Anne-Marie switched on the music and the lights. Then she stopped a moment and looked around.

Even on a wet night like tonight, she always had the same excited feeling at opening time. With the lights flashing, and the music playing, every ride on the fairground looked great.

And the dodgems look the best of all, thought Anne-Marie. Rick had the cars lined up now, seventeen of them standing waiting for their drivers. They were red and yellow, green and orange, purple and white. Each car had a big, black number on its side.

"Roll up!" shouted Rick. "Roll up now."

Anne-Marie went to stand beside him. They smiled at each other.

"Ride the dodgems!" shouted Anne-Marie. "Come and ride the dodgems now."

But only three or four people went hurrying by, their heads bent against the rain.

By half-past ten that night, Rick and Anne-Marie had only taken seven pounds. And the rain was heavier than ever.

"Why don't you two shut up shop?" said Anne-Marie's dad, hurrying past on his way home. "Everybody else has."

"Good idea," said Rick. "I'll turn the power off. Nobody will come now."

"Hang on a moment," said Anne-Marie. "Somebody is coming. Look."

Rick looked out into the darkness, his hand on the switch.

"Right," he said.

He bent down and pulled out the nearest car, the purple and white one with the number 9 on its side.

"Hi, there!" he said to the young woman who had just arrived. "Come to ride the dodgems, have you?"

Chapter 2

Eyes as Green as Glass

The young woman had long, fair hair. She was wearing a shiny, black raincoat and black boots.

"I've no money," she said, looking down at the car, then looking up at Rick. Anne-Marie saw her eyes were as green as glass.

Rick laughed.

"No problem," he said. "We were just closing anyway. Get in."

And almost before Anne-Marie could tell what was happening, the young woman had climbed into Car 9 and Rick had pushed it off.

Round and round the rink she drove, her hands gripping the wheel, her hair blowing in the wind, a little smile on her lips.

"All right?" shouted Rick as she went past.

"It's beautiful," she said. Her voice was very soft. "Come and join me."

"OK," said Rick.

He dropped into the nearest car. Suddenly Anne-Marie felt scared.

"Rick, don't!" she said. But Rick's car was already spinning off across the rink, racing after Car 9.

"Come and catch me," the young woman called, smiling at him.

CLANK! The lights went out, and the cars came to a stop in the middle of the rink.

"Oh, what's happened?" cried the young woman, looking round. She twisted the wheel this way and that.

"I've turned the power off," said Anne-Marie. "It's time to go home. Out you get."

Slowly, the young woman climbed out of the car. Her long hair hid her face. But Anne-Marie thought she saw her say something to Rick. And she thought Rick nodded and smiled. Then the young woman had slipped away into the darkness, and Rick was coming over to her.

"Time to go home," said Anne-Marie again.

Rick said nothing. But, later, when he and Anne-Marie were having supper in the caravan, Anne-Marie said, "Riding the dodgems without paying! The little madam!"

"Don't call her that," said Rick. "Her name's Kesta. That's what she told me. Her name is Kesta."

Chapter 3

The Most Beautiful Thing

After that, it seemed as if Kesta couldn't keep away from the dodgems. She didn't come every evening. Sometimes Anne-Marie didn't see her for three or four nights. Then she'd hope she'd never see her again. But Kesta always came back. Always.

One evening, it all became too much. For once, it was fine. The fairground was crowded. Plenty of people wanted to ride the dodgems. Rick and Anne-Marie were kept busy all evening. Anne-Marie had no time to think about Kesta. Then, just as a ride had started, she saw her.

Kesta was all alone, just like she always was, and she was out in the middle of the rink, driving Car 9. Just like she always was. She saw Anne-Marie looking at her and gave her a little smile.

Suddenly, Anne-Marie was very angry.

"Rick!" she shouted over the loud music.

Rick was dodging across the rink, on his way to sort out two boys whose car had got stuck. He looked back.

"What's SHE doing here?" Anne-Marie pointed at Car 9.

"What?" Rick pretended to cover his ears. "Can't hear you!"

Just then, three or four cars came round together, and Anne-Marie had to step back.

I'll turn the power off, she thought. Like I did last time. That will get rid of her. But she didn't dare do it with so many cars on the rink. The other punters would lose their ride. They might demand their money back.

She stood at the side, watching unhappily. The music banged and thudded. The punters laughed and screamed as their cars bumped against each other. Only Car 9 drove quietly round and round the rink without bumping. Kesta wasn't laughing. She wasn't screaming. She was just smiling to herself. Her green eyes were dreamy and far away.

Anne-Marie saw Rick on the far side of the rink. His arms were folded. He was staring at Kesta. Staring as if she was the most beautiful thing he'd ever seen.

I've had enough, thought Anne-Marie.

Chapter 4

Empty Road

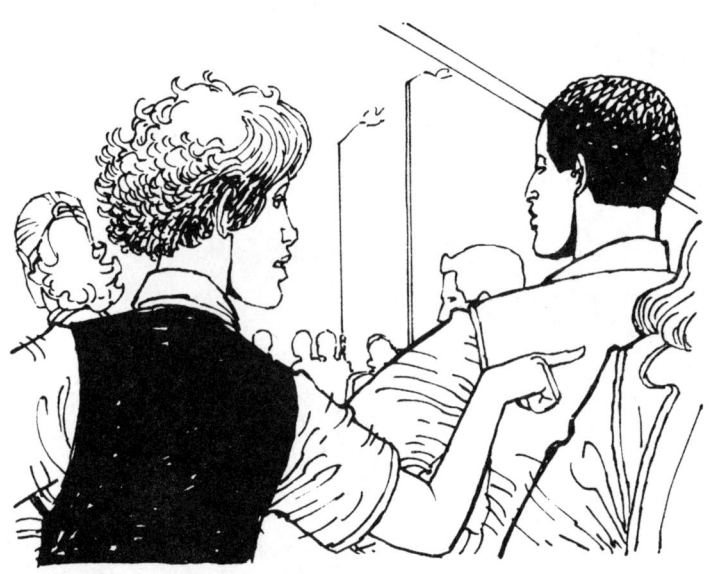

Anne-Marie pushed her way through the crowds.

"Tell her to go away!" she said to Rick. "Now!"

Slowly, Rick turned and looked at her.

"Who?" he asked.

"You know who."

Rick shrugged and said nothing. He was still watching Kesta.

"All the other punters pay for their rides," said Anne-Marie. "Why should you let Kesta ride free? You let her ride free, Rick, every time. Don't you?" She shook his arm. "Don't you, Rick?"

"Why shouldn't I give a free ride to a friend now and then?" said Rick.

Anne-Marie laughed angrily.

"She's not a friend," she said. "Do you know what I think? I think Kesta's got some hold over you."

But she was talking to herself. Rick had gone.

"I'm right," Anne-Marie whispered. "It's almost like a spell or something."

The ride was coming to an end.

"Next ride! Next ride!" Rick shouted. "All ready for the next ride!"

Everybody was climbing out of the cars. New people were coming forward. Anne-Marie was just in time to see Kesta vanishing into the crowd.

She had to know where Kesta came from. Without stopping to think, she followed her.

Most people who visited the fair came from the town. But Kesta didn't go that way. She turned the other way and set off into the dark. Anne-Marie hurried along behind her.

As usual, Kesta was wearing her black raincoat. Anne-Marie could hardly see her. But her long fair hair showed up in the moonlight.

Where could she be going? There were no lights anywhere. No houses. And why was she in such a hurry? She was almost running now. Her feet made no sound on the road.

Anne-Marie was out of breath. Kesta was getting further and further ahead. She was nearly at the bridge over the river. Anne-Marie couldn't keep up. She'd have to go back to the fair soon, or there would be more trouble with Rick.

But there was no need for Anne-Marie to worry. At the bridge she stood for a minute to get her breath back. She could see the road ahead from there, clear and bright in the moonlight. Clear and bright and empty.

Kesta had gone.

Chapter 5

Final Week

It was a very wet summer.

"I'll be glad when we move on," said Anne-Marie.

Big red notices had gone up on the fairground, saying 'FINAL WEEK'. On Saturday night, they would pack up and go.

But, if Anne-Marie was glad, Rick wasn't. Anne-Marie knew why. It was because of Kesta.

Now, in this final week, Kesta began to come to the fair every night. And she stayed later and later, long after everyone else had gone. She and Rick spent a lot of time talking together in low voices. And Rick had even begun to stop anyone else driving Car 9.

"No, not that one," Anne-Marie heard him tell someone. "That car's broken."

It wasn't, of course. There was nothing wrong with it when Kesta drove it. Except –

Except that when Kesta drove it, Car 9 never, ever, touched anything. And nothing touched Car 9.

Why hadn't Anne-Marie noticed before? Watching from the side, she began to see. And it made her cold all over. It was weird.

Sometimes one of the other drivers would head right for Car 9. Then, at the last second, the other driver's car would somehow swerve away. And Car 9 would go on its way untouched, with Kesta still smiling that secret, cool, little smile. And the other driver was left staring, not knowing quite what had happened.

It was as if Kesta had some secret power over Car 9.

"Oh, come on, Saturday, come ON!" Anne-Marie whispered to herself. After Saturday she would leave Kesta behind.

It rained and rained.

"They say there'll be floods at the bridge," Anne-Marie's dad said.

Saturday night came. Kesta came to ride the dodgems one last time. Anne-Marie didn't try to stop her. Not even when Kesta drove Car 9 all evening. Not even when Rick sat beside her. It didn't matter. Nothing mattered on this last night.

But when Kesta left, Rick left with her. Without a word to Anne-Marie, who was shutting up the pay-desk. She looked up and saw them walking off together in the rain.

She couldn't believe it. Rick wouldn't do that.

But he had.

For a minute, she stood staring, her heart thudding. Then she began to run.

Chapter 6

Waking

She followed them down the road, towards the bridge. She had no coat, and the rain beat down on her. She could see them in front, their heads close together.

She heard the river before she got there. The water was roaring like a lion in a cage. She saw Kesta and Rick nearly at the bridge.

"Look out!" she shouted. "The floods ..."

Even as she shouted, she found herself up to her knees in icy water.

"Oh! Oh!" She struggled to get back on her feet. Somewhere another voice was shouting too. Rick's voice.

"Help me! Help me! Help!"

Anne-Marie fought her way through the water. She saw Rick in the river, struggling. And she saw Kesta there too, pulling at him.

"NO!"

Anne-Marie knew now. The river was Kesta's home. She would pull Rick down under the water with her, and he would be gone for ever.

Somehow she reached Rick, gasping for breath. As she tried to pull him out of the water, she saw Kesta's face one last time. Her wet hair was floating, her green eyes glinting. And still that little, cool smile on her lips. Then she'd gone.

Anne-Marie hardly knew that strong arms were helping them from the water, lifting them to safety.

"These terrible floods ... Careful now," said voices around her. She heard the sound of an ambulance coming. "You'll be all right," someone said. "You'll both be all right now."

Kesta had gone. It was just Rick and Anne-Marie now.

Anne-Marie looked at Rick. She saw his eyes begin to open and look at her. As if he was waking up from a long, bad dream.

"Anne-Marie?" he said.

Yes, they'd both be all right now.